Contents

UNIT 1

Out and about

NATIONAL EXPRESS RAPIDE

Code **D** – daily

Service Number	**711**	**709**	**710**
Days of Operation	**D**	**D**	**D**
NEWCASTLE U TYNE, Coach Stn	0750	0950	1150
Durham Bus Stn	↓	1020	↓
SUNDERLAND, Park Lane Bus Stn	0820	↓	1220
MIDDLESBROUGH, Bus Stn	0900	↓	1300
BIRMINGHAM, Coach Stn Digbeth	1205	1410	1605

days of operation – the days that the buses are running
stn – station

1.1

Read the timetable above. Then answer the questions.

1 *a)* What time does the first bus from Newcastle to Birmingham leave?

____

b) What time does it arrive in Birmingham?

____

c) What will the service number of this bus be?

____

2 When does the 1150 bus from Newcastle arrive at Middlesbrough?

____

3 What time is the bus from Durham to Birmingham?

____

4 Write down the full words for Stn and D.

____

1.2

SB

PAGES
94–99
104–106

Copy the passage below, putting in capital letters, full stops and commas. Set it out as you think best.

dear sir on monday may 4th i caught the 9.50 bus from london which should have arrived in bristol at 13.05 however the coach broke down and i was two hours late for a meeting i would like my money refunded and an apology yours faithfully

1.3

Check how well you know the 24-hour clock. Fill in the chart below.

1400	2 pm	two o'clock
0900		
1605		
1150		
1815		
2030		

Alexander's end is gold and rainbow

by DAVE BARTON
Chief Sportswriter

BARROW-in-Furness does not have much going for it these days. The town used to build ships. Now this has almost stopped. It does, however, have Britain's top female cross-country mountain bike rider.

Not so long ago, the 26-year-old had to stop working in the shipyard, but Caroline Alexander is not the sort to hang around. She has been National Mountain Bike Champion for the past four years and the cyclo-cross supremo for the last two.

It has not all been easy for Alexander. She hurt her back in New Zealand and then became ill with a virus. But she has trained hard.

Good rides at Plymouth, in Rome next Saturday and in Germany will give her an Olympic place. Now a gold in Atlanta would *really* be a plus for Barrow-in-Furness.

Rainbow warrior: Caroline Alexander, who is training for the World Champion's rainbow jersey in Plymouth this weekend.

Adapted from: *The Western Morning News*

1.4

Read the newspaper article opposite. Then answer the questions.

1 *a)* What is the full name of the girl in the article?

____

b) How old is she?

____

c) Where does she live?

____

d) What is she famous for?

____

2 Write down two things that have made life difficult for her.

____

____

____

3 What used to be made in the town that Caroline lives in?

____

4 What would Caroline like to win at the Olympics?

____

5 Who wrote the article?

____

1.5

Write down three questions you could ask Caroline. Pick questions that you think people might like to know the answer to.

____

____

____

____

descent – going down hill

1.6

Look at the map opposite. Then answer the questions.

1 *a)* What big sporting event is this map telling you about?

____

b) In which town is it taking place?

____

2 What is the name of the river on the map?

____

3 What happens at number 1?

____

4 If you cycle from 1 to 2, is it uphill or down? Say how you know.

____

____

5 What might make cycling difficult at number 4?

____

____

6 Cycling from 5 to the river, is it uphill or down? Say how you know.

____

7 What does this sign tell you? 

____

8 What will the cyclists be doing at number 11?

____

9 Where would you stand if you were going to watch the race? Say why.

____

____

STAGE 9: PLYMOUTH

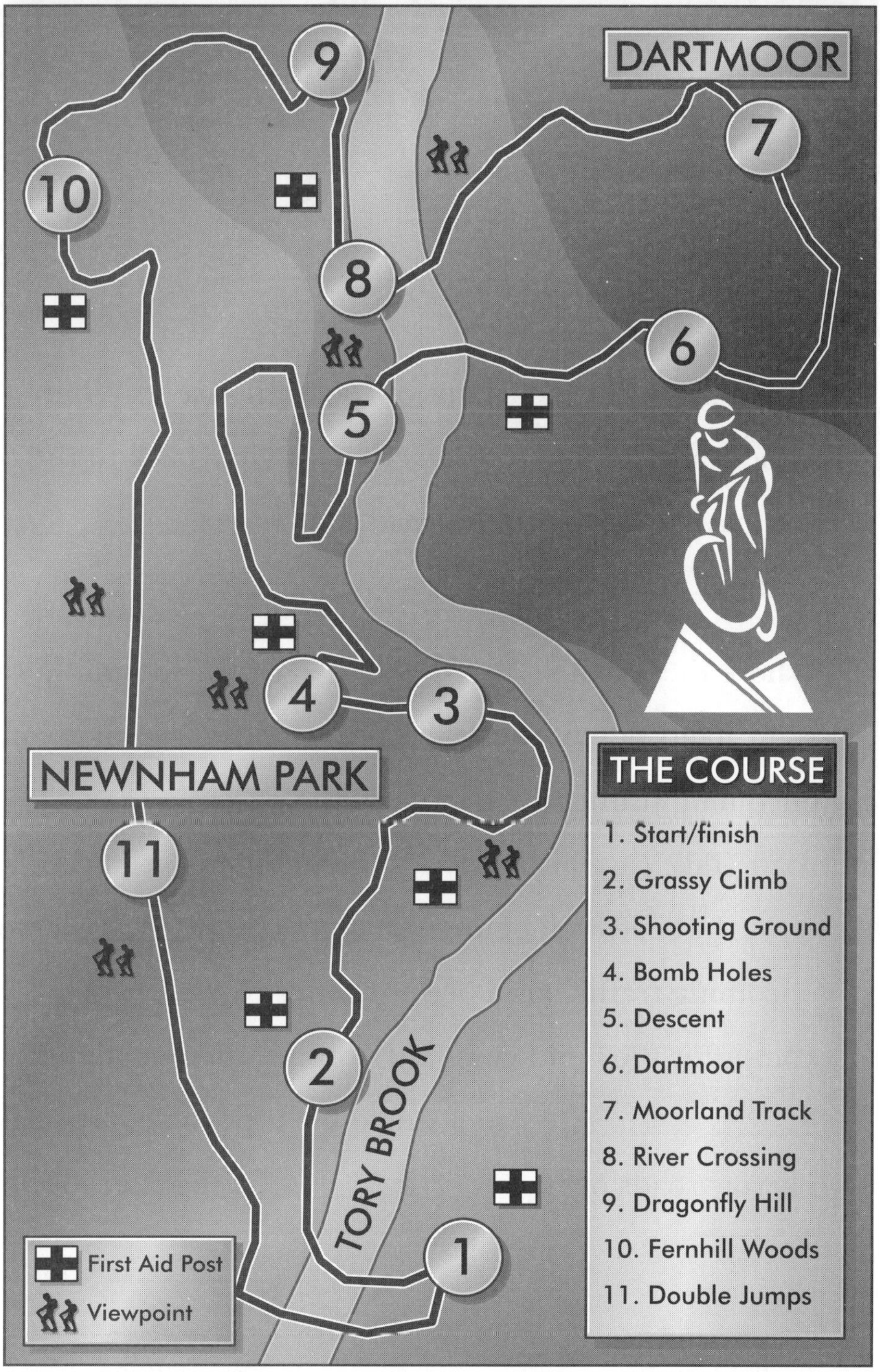

1.7

Read the passage. Then fill each gap with one of the words from the box below.

pedestrian – someone who walks

When there is a pavement or footpath, use it. Where possible avoid walking next to the kerb with your back to the traffic. If you have to step into the road, watch out ________________ traffic.

Where there is no ________________ or footpath, walk on the right-hand side of the ________________ so that you can see oncoming traffic. Keep close to the ________________ of the road. Take care at sharp right-hand bends; it may be safer to cross the road well before ________________ reach one so that oncoming traffic has a better chance of ________________ you. After the bend cross back to face the oncoming traffic. ________________ in a single file if possible, especially on narrow roads or in ________________ light.

From the *Highway Code*

seeing	road	walk	you
pavement	poor	side	for

1.8

Use the diagrams below.

1 Draw and label the three diagrams to make it clear how you should walk:

a) when there is a pavement

b) when there is no pavement

c) when there is no pavement and a sharp right-hand bend.

a)

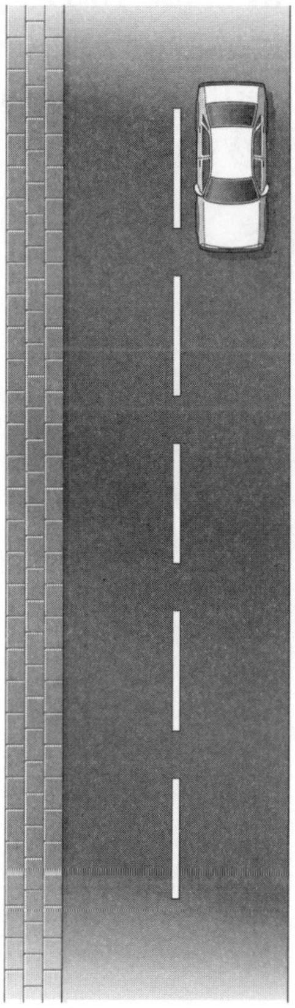

b)

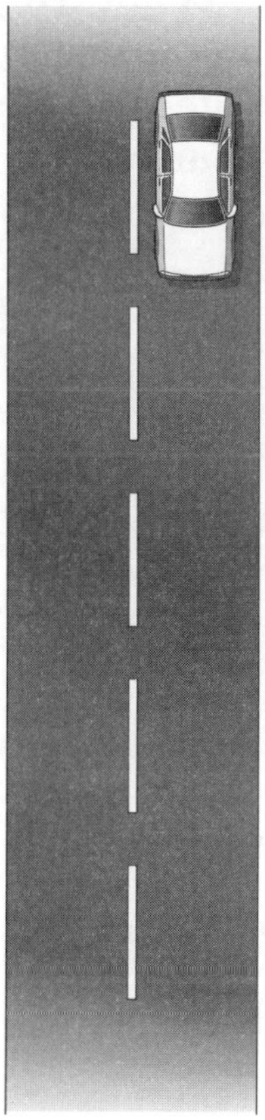

c)

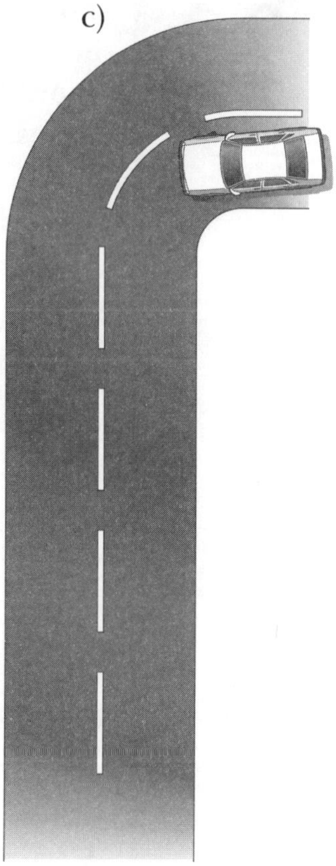

1.9

Make a list of tips to help a nine-year-old cross the road safely. There is no pedestrian crossing.

UNIT 2

Fit to eat

2.1

The instructions below tell you how to make an IRISH TEA-BREAD, but they are in the wrong order. Work out the order you think they should be in. Write your answers by putting the number 1–7 in the boxes. The first one has been done for you.

A	In the morning add 2 cups of flour and an egg.	☐
B	Put on a wire rack to cool.	☐
C	Turn on the oven to 220°C.	☐
D	Leave to soak overnight.	☐
E	Serve with butter.	☐
F	Put the mixture in a large loaf tin and cook at 220°C.	☐
G	Mix together 500 g of dried fruit, a cup of dark brown sugar and a cup of black tea.	1

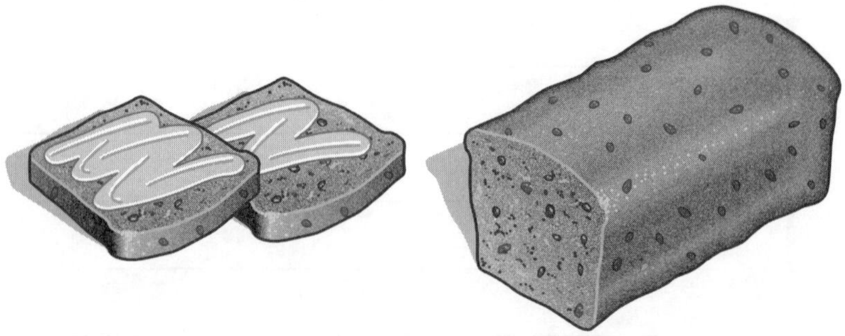

2.2

SB

PAGES 115–118

The names of some of the people who work for a supermarket are given below. Rewrite the names in the spaces on the right, putting the names in alphabetical order.

Neale F. ____________________

Tuson R. ____________________

Din A. ____________________

Kumar M.S. ____________________

Jackson L. ____________________

Wood G. ____________________

Turner C. ____________________

Neil H. ____________________

Kumar P. ____________________

Bull S. ____________________

2.3

SB

PAGES 107–109

TRF

PAGE 110

Fill in the blanks in the shopping list below. Use the word at the end of each line but make it plural.

1 Three packets of ________________ (crisp)

2 A bag of ________________ (potato)

3 Four ________________ (peach)

4 A kilo of ________________ (cherry)

5 Two ________________ of bread (loaf)

6 A kilo of ________________ (tomato)

2.4

Read the survey (pages 14, 15 and 16). Then fill in the answers.

FOOD AND HEALTH SURVEY

Q1 **How often do you eat fresh fruit?**
PLEASE TICK ONE BOX

- At least once a day ☐
- 3–6 times a week ☐
- 1–2 times a week ☐
- Less often ☐
- Never ☐

Q2 **How often do you eat fresh or freshly cooked vegetables?**
PLEASE TICK ONE BOX

- At least once a day ☐
- 3–6 times a week ☐
- 1–2 times a week ☐
- Less often ☐
- Never ☐

Q3 **How often do you eat fried food?**
PLEASE TICK ONE BOX

- At least once a day ☐
- 3–6 times a week ☐
- 1–2 times a week ☐
- Less often ☐
- Never ☐

FOOD AND HEALTH SURVEY

Q4 How often do you eat each of the following types of meat?
PLEASE TICK ONE BOX FOR EACH TYPE

	At least once a day	**3–6 times a week**	**1–2 times a week**	**Less often**	**Never**
Red meat (e.g. beef, pork, lamb)	❑	❑	❑	❑	❑
Processed meat (e.g. sausages, beefburgers, meat pies)	❑	❑	❑	❑	❑
Poultry (e.g. chicken, turkey)	❑	❑	❑	❑	❑
Grilled meat of any kind	❑	❑	❑	❑	❑

Q5 How often do you add salt to your food while eating your meal?
PLEASE TICK ONE BOX

All meals	❑
Most meals	❑
Some meals	❑
Occasional meals	❑
Never	❑

Q6 How often do you eat sweets or confectionery (including chocolate)?
PLEASE TICK ONE BOX

At least once a day	❑
3–6 times a week	❑
1–2 times a week	❑
Less often	❑

confectionery – sweets

FOOD AND HEALTH SURVEY

Q7 **For each of the places listed below, do you think smoking should be banned?**
PLEASE TICK ONE BOX FOR EACH TYPE OF PUBLIC PLACE

	Smoking should be completely banned	**Smoking should be banned in some areas only**	**Smoking should be allowed in all areas**	**Don't know**
Public transport	☐	☐	☐	☐
Restaurants and cafés	☐	☐	☐	☐
Pubs	☐	☐	☐	☐
Cinemas, theatres, etc.	☐	☐	☐	☐
Workplaces	☐	☐	☐	☐
Schools	☐	☐	☐	☐
Colleges	☐	☐	☐	☐

2.5

Pick one of the places listed in Q7 in the questionnaire above. Write down the reasons why you think smoking should be banned or not banned in this place.

2.6

Read the passage below. Fill in each blank with one of the words from the box at the bottom of the page.

EXERCISE

If you're not very active now, your first step to getting fitter is to walk more. Why __________________ in a bus queue or sit in a traffic jam when you could __________________ or cycle part of the way?

When __________________ walk, walk faster. Walking briskly for 20 or 30 __________________ two or three times a __________________ will soon help to get you fit. It is the perfect __________________ .

Use the stairs instead of the lift. Climbing stairs is a good way of __________________ your leg muscles strong.

keeping	minutes	you	walk	week	exercise	stand

UNIT 3

For sale

3.1

Look at the diagram opposite. Then answer the questions.

1 *a)* Where is most of the heat lost from a house?

____

b) Which place loses the second most amount of heat?

____

2 Write down two ways in which heat is lost from an outside door.

____

____

3 Write down two reasons why windows might lose heat.

____

____

4 If it was possible to stop all of the heat going from the roof, outside doors and windows, how much heat could you save?

____

3.2

Make a list of some of the ways you could stop heat from going out of the doors, windows and roof.

____

____

____

____

____

THE WAY HEAT CAN BE LOST

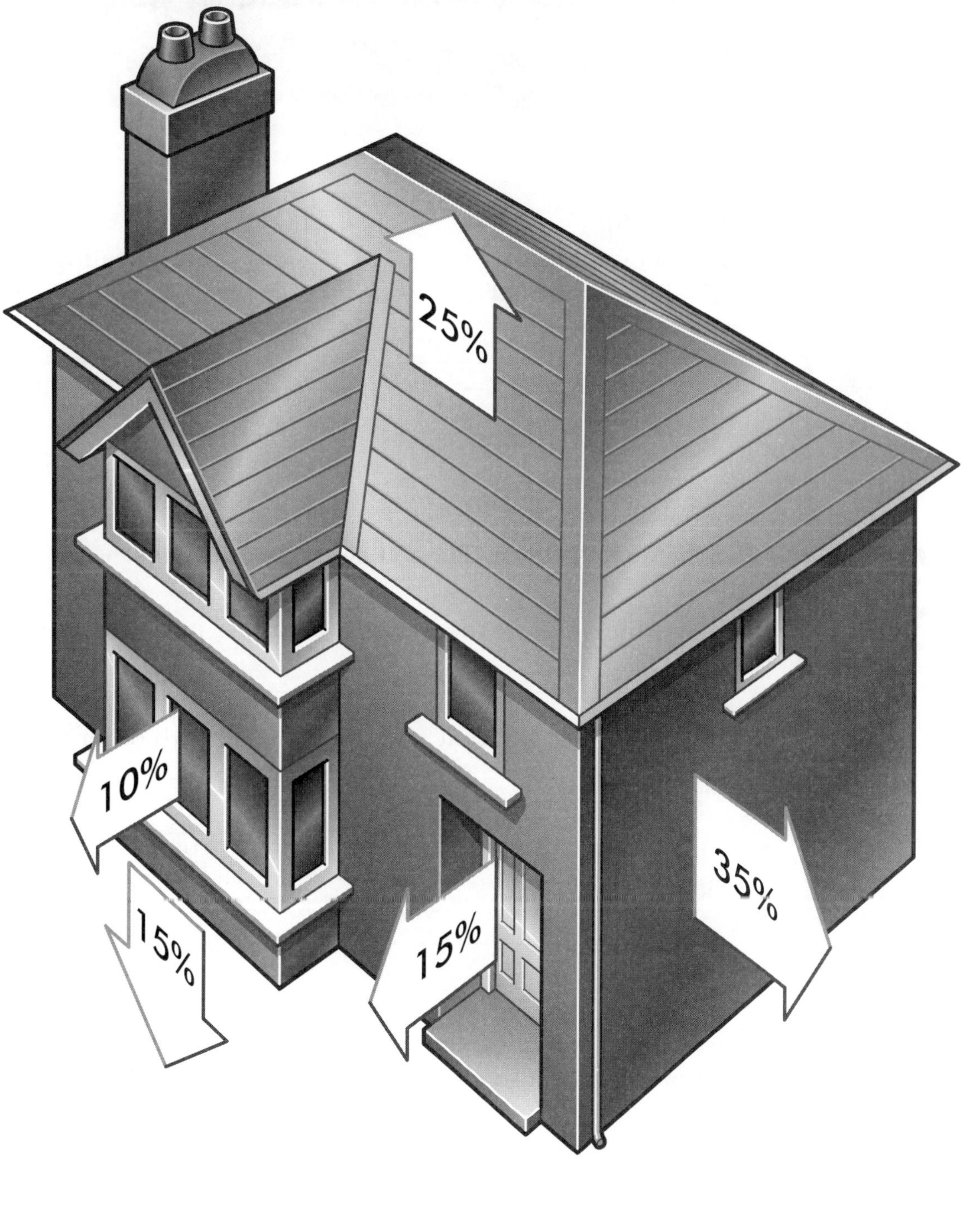

ALDERNEY EDGE dbl room in shared hse. n.s. GCH F/F £45 pw Tel 46098137 evgs & w/e

dbl - **d**ou**bl**e	**hse** – house
n.s. – no smoking	**GCH** – gas central heating
F/F – fully furnished	**pw** – each week
evgs – evenings	**w/e** – weekends

3.3

Read the details above. Then answer the questions.

1 What is the name of the place where there is a room to rent?

____

2 What word tells you that you will be living with other people?

____

3 Name two places in the house that other people will use as well as you.

____

____

4 Write down two good things about living with others and two things that might not be so good.

____

____

____

____

3.4

Read the advertisement on page 20 again. Then write out the advertisement in full.

3.5

SB

PAGES
94–99
104–106

Copy the passage below putting in capital letters, full stops and commas. Set out your work as you think best.

dear mrs denton i am writing to inform you of a change of address i am moving to york on march 7th the new address is 24 wilton road york yo1 2dp please let mr potts know yours sincerely

James Fisher

ESTATE AGENCY

INCORPORATED VALUER and AUCTIONEER

64 Broad Street Portsmouth PO6 3BT
Tel: 01705 654321 Fax: 01705 123456

TENANT APPLICATION FORM

1 NAME ______________________________

2 PRESENT ADDRESS ______________________________

____

____

3 TEL NO (Home) ______________________________ (Work) ______________

4 How soon do you wish your tenancy to start?

____

5 What type or size of property do you seek?

____

6 Who will occupy the property?

____

7 Do you have any pets you may wish to bring into the property?

____

8 Do you require furnished, part-furnished or unfurnished property?

____

9 Maximum monthly rent you are prepared to pay: (underline)

£200 £250 £300 £350 over £400

10 Name and address of employer (from whom references will be taken)

____

____

____

Name of contact: ______________________________

SIGNED: ______________________________

DATE: ______________________________

tenant – someone who rents property	**tenancy** – renting
seek – look	**occupy** – live in
maximum – the most	

3.6

Read the form on page 22. Then answer the questions.

1 Why do you think a landlord may want to know if someone is going to keep pets?

____

____

2 Why do you think the landlord wants to get references from an employer?

____

____

3.7

Read the passage below. Then fill in the form on page 22 using Tasmin's details.

Tasmin Daily is looking for a fully furnished, one-bedroomed flat. She works at the Red Lion Hotel. Now her boss, Linda Small, wants her to go away for a training week.

Tasmin asks you to look after her cat for her while she is away. She also asks you to fill in a form for rented property for her. At the moment she is living in lodgings at 12 Ash Avenue, Portsmouth, PO3 5LK, but she would like to move as soon as possible. She does not want to pay more than £300 a month for the flat and would prefer to pay £250. The hotel she works in is in Oakfield Drive, Portsmouth. The telephone number is 01705 60000. She is not on the phone at her lodgings.

Welcome to

CLASSIFIED

QUICK GUIDE

Family Announcements	Section **A**
Sales and Wants	Section **B**
Sell it Coupon	Section **B**
Holidays	Section **C**
Situations Vacant	Section **D**
Property	Section **E**
Motors	Section **F**
Entertainments	Section **G**

announcement – telling people something
situations – jobs
vacant – here it means there is a job
property – houses, flats
motors – cars, motorbikes, etc.

3.8

Read advertisements 1–5 on the opposite page.
Work out where you would find each advertisement using the QUICK GUIDE above.

Advertisement 1 in section ____________

Advertisement 2 in section ____________

Advertisement 3 in section ____________

Advertisement 4 in section ____________

Advertisement 5 in section ____________

1 **BIRD TABLE** With roof
Free standing. £16 Tel 0161 910000

2 **HELICOPTER FLIGHT** over Newcastle.
Only £36. Ring 0161 795000

3 **GATESHEAD** Nr Park. Furn
rooms £38 pw Tel 492048

4 **METRO** Van "E" Regstr.
MoT to May 26th
Tel (0161 987321)

5 **PART TIME** kitchen staff
wanted evenings and
weekends
Tel 0161 874051

3.9

Pick TWO of the advertisements that you might be interested in. Write three questions to ask when you make the phone call, for example:

Advertisement 4: What colour is the van?

Questions — Advertisement ☐

1 ______________________________

____

2 ______________________________

____

3 ______________________________

____

Questions — Advertisement ☐

1 ______________________________

____

2 ______________________________

____

3 ______________________________

____

3.10

Read page 27. Then answer the questions.

1 How much does it cost to put in a FOR SALE advertisement?

___

2 Which newspapers will the advertisement go into?

___

___

3 What three things can you not sell using this form?

___

4 What is the latest time to get your advertisement to the paper so that it will be in the paper that week?

___

5 Write down the words on the form that tell you how many words you can use for the advertisement.

___

6 What details MUST you have in your advertisement?

___

7 Write down the address where the filled in form must be sent.

___

___

___

3.11

Fill in the form opposite, using your own details.
Sell something you do not want or pick one of the following.

bicycle	rabbit hutch	doll's house
videos	hamster cage	games

FREE!

You can sell your unwanted items *ABSOLUTELY FREE* in the *Express Advertiser and Times Newspapers*

Just fill in the coupon below and return it to us before Monday 1pm and we'll guarantee it's in for free!

You can sell anything *(apart from property, cars and pets).*
When filling in the coupon remember to include your address or telephone number in the grid and also the price(s) of the article(s) you are selling.

Please write your advertisement in the grid below.
One word for each space (maximum 20 words).

TEL NO:

Name ....

Address...

....

....

........................Post code..............................Tel No..

Post it to: ***FREE PRIVATE ADS*, Express Advertiser and Times, Wood Street, Stockport SK3 0AB**
or simply drop in the coupon at your local Express Advertiser Office

guarantee – a promise

maximum – the biggest number

UNIT 4

Heads and tails

4.1

You work for Crunch Pet Foods. Tomorrow you have to deliver a parcel to Mr Let for your boss. Mr Let works in another part of the country. He is going to meet you at the train station. Write down the message you leave on his answer phone. Give your name, say when you will arrive and what you will be wearing, etc. so that he can recognise you.

____

____

____

____

____

____

4.2

The abbreviations below all come from addresses in a telephone book. Write down what each abbreviation stands for. Use the words in the box to help you.

dr	drive	la	______	st	______
pk	______	wlk	______	clo	______
av	______	sq	______	rd	______
pl	______	gdns	______	cres	______

park	square	close	lane
drive ✓	gardens	walk	road
street	crescent	avenue	place

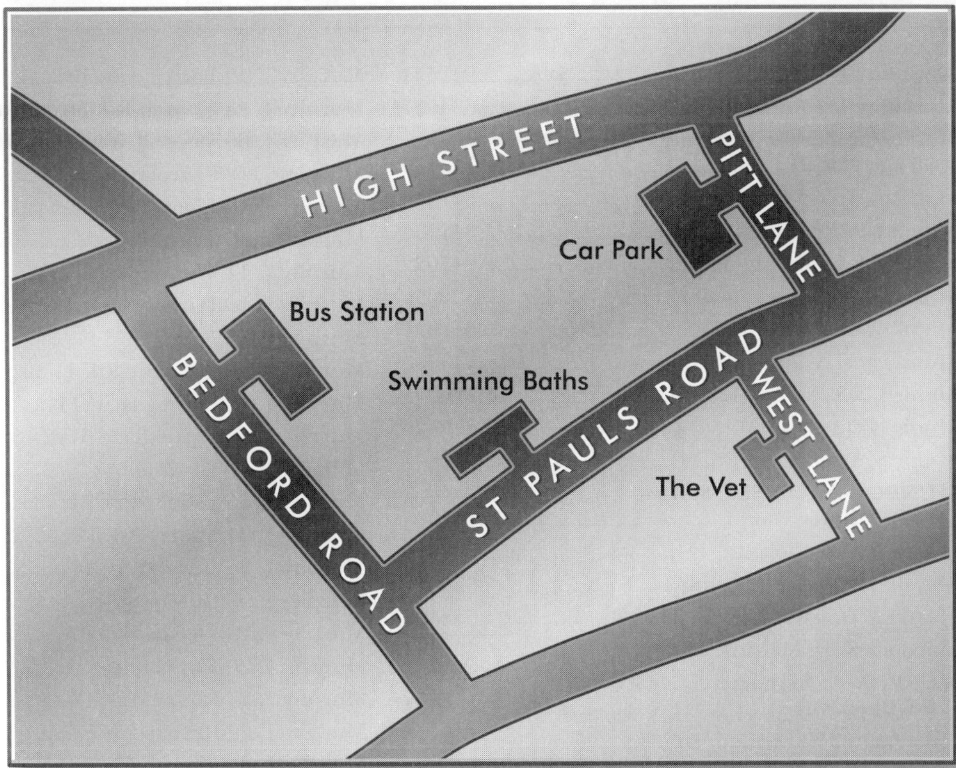

4.3

Look at the map.

1 Write down the directions for someone who wants to go:

a) from the car park to the vet

___

___

___

b) from the bus station to the High Street

___

___

c) from the bus station to the swimming baths

___

___

d) from the vet to the bus station.

___

___

___

Mulvanny B, 12 Harding Rd, 4 948554
Mulvanny J, 13 Bute Rd, 10 634937
Munday & Barker, Vetn Surg
90 Chaytor Pl 713200
Munday W, 105 Darebury St, 21 821010
Munday R, 8 Orton Rd, 11 841135
Mundy M, 24 Grange Pk 947622
Mundy P, 36 Brompton St, 14 326055
Munif A, 24 Sledmere Dr, 11 631021
Munif N, 17 Vernon Rd, 16 443290
Munir L, 62 Barlow St, 19 520901
Munir N, 14 Elvate Way, 8 436826
Munir S, 4A Finchley St, 14 329311
MUNROE & RAMSEY, Solrs -
557 Mulliner Way 443208
Murch B, 107 Viola Rd, 11 637026
Murch T, 101 Cadogan Rd, 14 320346
Murdock H, 54 Stokes Rd, 11 638802
Murdock S, 18 Marcliffe Pk, 19 537243
MURPHY A, Newsagts,
3 Willow Way 426571
Murphy A, 3 Turner Rd, 18 683130
Murphy A, 25 Kings St, 16 723902
Murphy A, 98b Austell St, 16 718154
Murphy B, 325 Aden Dr, 12 890781
Murphy B, 14 Fairfield Rd, 1 321807
Murphy B, 10 Stelling Rd, 18 693772
Murphy B, 101 John Rd, ...749926
Murphy B, 77 Grasmere Rd, 12 885243
Murphy B, 12 Furness St, 14 328023
Murphy C.G, 3 Finchley St, 14 326689
Murphy C.H, 13 Deeroak Dr, 18 684008
Murphy C.J, 8 Bealey Rd, ...363230
Murphy C.J, 12 Bath Way, 16 473209
Murphy C.L, 46 Manley St 368882
Murphy C.M, 10 Hallows Way 815425
Murphy C.R, 90 Mayan Way, 3 661021
Murphy C.W, 89 Queens St, 10 649355
Murphy D.A, 142 Reeves St, 21 824792
Murphy D.B, 18 Edward Rd, 9 432701
Murphy D.C, 47 Cheadle Rd, 18 679990
Murphy D.C, 21 Calver Passage, 10 652330
Murphy E, 43 Irlam St, Flixton 239726
Murphy F, 31 Sussex Rd, 7 412254
Murphy G, 5 Royal Way 327822
Murphy G, 26 Rigel Sq, 7 416410
Murphy G, 83 Slam Rd 481021
Murphy G, 59 Stopford Rd, 11 638323
Murphy H, 26 Chaytor Way, 10 635354
Murphy H, 90 Beech St 426681
Murphy I, 19 Kilsby Passage, 10 652822
Murphy J, 6 Riverside, 7 412827
Murphy J, 35 Churton Way, 14 341012
Murphy J, 40 Portville St, 19 522333
Murphy J, 33 Church Rd, Stretford 891020
Murphy J, 66 Deverill Way, 18 676865
Murphy J, 123 Nicolas St 412253
Murphy J, 10 Egerton St, 14 329032
Murphy J, 36 Trust St, 18 697625
Murphy J, 11 Wilmslow St 574475
Murphy J, 16 Darley Way, 21 863497
Murphy J, 14 Brook St, 14 683388
Murphy J, 99 Manipur Rd, 11 631276
Murphy J, 113 Princess St, 14 314026
Murphy J, 67B Woodland Way, 18 674088
Murphy J, 61 St Austell St 512245
Murphy J, 6 Ansdell Way, 21 815322
Murphy J, 24 Milner Rd, 16 729067
Murphy J, 5 Audrey Way, 18 664129
Murphy J, 67 Gowan St, 16 723310
Murphy J, 23 Weedall Way, 5 987608
Murphy J, 20 Farrnat St, 12 895574
Murphy J, 24 Ripon Way, 18 683432
Murphy J, 20 Reynard St 443542
Murphy J, 25 Alcomb Rd, 14 327800
Murphy J.A, 5 Prout Rd 985912
Murphy J.A, 35 Heston Dv, 1 322148
Murphy J.B, 4 Brailsford St, 14 354467
Murphy J.C, 5 Platt Hill, 14 237023
Murphy J.M, 67 Cromwell St 398717
Murphy K, 14A Kinsdale St, 18 679572
Murphy K.M & Murphy, L, Dent Surg -
30 Norwood Sq 539723
Murphy M, 21 Spean Passage 379020
Murphy M.A, 204 Dalton Rd, 10 618142
Murphy M.A, 5 Lime Sq, 12 889987
Murphy M.A, 10 Repton Gdns 282909
Murphy M.R & Sons, Flor -
6 Barton Wlk 832484
Murphy M.S, 8 Firwood Wlk 679811
Murphy N, 10 Clough St, 9 465460
Murphy P, 9 Far Hill 341821
Murphy P, 31 Emery Av, 13 624007
Murphy R, 200 Heath Av 327981
Murphy R, 31 Alam St, 19 529901
Murphy S, 83 Conway St 983343
Murphy S, 6 Barnard Dr, 21 868484
Murphy S, 10 Linden Gdns, 19 549244
Murphy T, 6 Rona Passage 434412
Murphy W, 21 Flamingo Dr 273819
Murphy W, 6 Thornley Hill, Nrth 309026
Murray A, 20 Shrewsbury St, 16 710991
MURRAY HOUSE HOTEL Compton St 609434
Murray I, 100 Kings St, 16 725222

Vetn Surg – veterinary surgeon, vet
Solrs – solicitors
Newsagts – newsagents, a shop that sells newspapers
Dent Surg – dental surgeon, dentist
Flor – florist, someone who sells flowers

4.4

Answer the questions below. They are about page 30.

1 Write down the address and phone number of the dentist on page 30.

____

2 You are trying to find the phone number of a friend who has moved. His name is Mark Adrian Murphy. You do not know the full address but you know his house is number 10. Write out his address and phone number in full.

____

____

3 You want to order some flowers. Write down the phone number of the shop.

____

4 Write down the phone number and address of the vet in full.

____

____

5 What is the job of:

a) Munroe and Ramsey?

____

b) A Murphy, Willow Way?

____

4.5

SB PAGES 115–118

Four new names need to be added to page 30. Draw arrows on the page opposite to show where each of the names below should go.

a) Mundy J
b) Murphy C.P
c) Murphy M.W
d) Mumford P

NORTHUMBRIA'S STUNNING NEW ATTRACTION

Discover the thrilling world beneath the waves.

Come face to face with thousands of fascinating sea creatures.

Experience the thrill of the deep sea dive.

Journey through the underwater tunnel; surrounded by gallons of water and sinister sharks.

It's a Different Adventure Every Time!

Tynemouth Sea Life Centre, Grand Parade, Tynemouth.
Telephone (0191) 257 6100

4.6 **Read the advertisement above. Then answer the questions.**

1 What will you see at this centre?

___

2 Explain how it is possible to 'Walk underwater and stay dry'.

3 Why do you think it says: 'It's a different adventure every time'?

4 *a)* Write down two words from the advertisement that describe the sea creatures. ______

b) Which word best describes how you might feel? ______

5 Write down one piece of information that is not in the advertisement.

6 Write down one reason why a five-year-old might be frightened to go to the sea centre.

4.7

SB
PAGE 126

Imagine you are on holiday on Tyneside and have been to the sea centre. Write a postcard home telling them about your holiday and describing what it was like at the sea centre. Fill in the address, etc.

Sea Life Centre, Grand Parade, Tynemouth.

UNIT 5

Take the weather with you

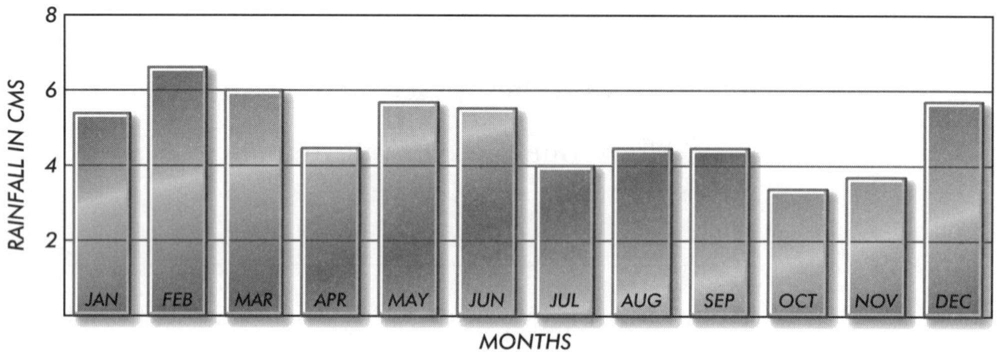

RAINFALL IN GREENWICH

5.1

Look at the graph. Then answer the questions.

1 Which was the wettest month?

____

2 Which month had the least rain?

____

3 How much rain fell in July?

____

4 Write down three important ways we use water.

____

5 Write out the months of the year in order.

1 ________ 2 ________ 3 ________

4 ________ 5 ________ 6 ________

7 ________ 8 ________ 9 ________

10 ________ 11 ________ 12 ________

Lemon Ice

SERVES 6–8

3 large juicy lemons
850 ml ($3\frac{3}{4}$ cups) water
200 g (1 cup) fine sugar
2 egg whites

Peel the rind from the lemons with a potato peeler and squeeze the lemons. Put the water, lemon rind, juice and sugar into a saucepan. Bring to the boil, stirring until the sugar has dissolved. Simmer for another five minutes. Then pour the mixture through a strainer, into a cold bowl. Let the mixture cool down.

Pour the mixture into ice-cube freezer trays (with the ice-cube dividers taken away). Cover with foil. Put into the freezing compartment of the fridge. Leave until nearly frozen.

Beat the egg whites until they are stiff. Take the mixture from the fridge and mix it well. Then add the egg whites and mix again. Pour the mixture into a plastic box with a lid. Leave to freeze.

5.2

Read the recipe above. Then make a list of <u>everything</u> you need to make lemon ice, for example, fridge.

Gas

FOR ALL CUSTOMER SERVICES AND EMERGENCIES

■ **Find your Map Area Number**

Use the telephone number shown for your Map Area to call us for the cost of a local call

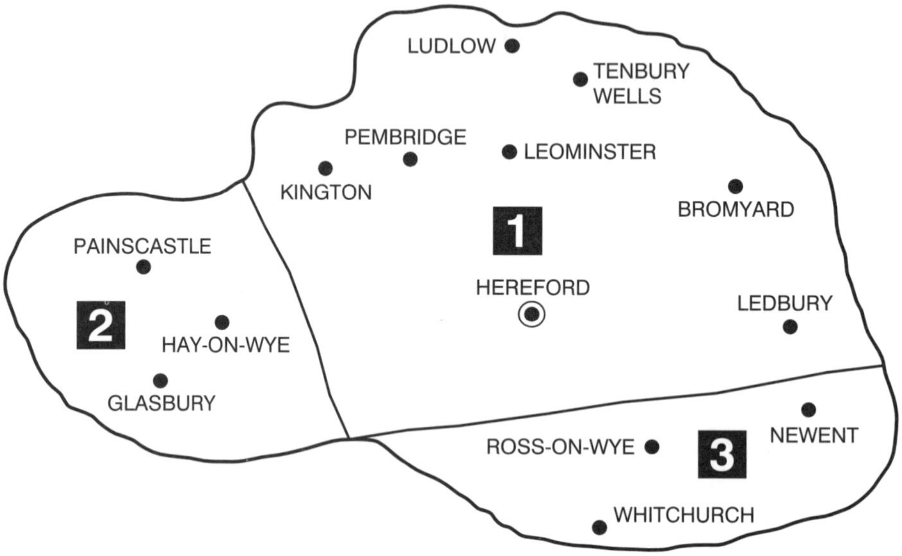

WE PROVIDE A 24 HOUR SERVICE FOR GAS ESCAPES AND URGENT CALLS

MAP AREA 1	MAP AREA 2	MAP AREA 3
Gas Escape Calls 0345 333 888	**Gas Escape Calls 0345 444 040**	**Gas Escape Calls 01452 309 990**
Gas Bill Enquiries 0345 212 123	Gas Bill Enquiries 0345 717 111	Gas Bill Enquiries 0345 959 497

5.3

Read the details on page 36. Then answer the questions.

1 If you live in Ledbury, what is your area number?

2 Write down the names of the towns in area 2.

3 You live in Ludlow. What number should you phone if you have a gas escape?

4 *a)* What number should you ring if you have a gas leak and live in Whitchurch?

b) Would there be someone to answer your call if you rang in the middle of the night? Write down the words that tell you this.

5 You live in Kington. Write down the number you should phone if you are unhappy about your gas bill.

5.4

The words in the sentences below are in the wrong order. Write them out in the order you think best, putting in capital letters and full stops.

1 off supply meter the the at gas Turn

2 gas windows to doors the of rid get Open and

3 use smoke flames Do naked not or

4 not switches on electric off or Do turn

UNIT 6

Ready for work

6.1

Write out the alphabet in capital letters.

____ ____ ____ ____ ____ ____ ____ ____ ____

____ ____ ____ ____ ____ ____ ____ ____ ____

____ ____ ____ ____ ____ ____ ____ ____

6.2

Write out the alphabet in lower case letters.

____ ____ ____ ____ ____ ____ ____ ____ ____

____ ____ ____ ____ ____ ____ ____ ____ ____

____ ____ ____ ____ ____ ____ ____ ____

6.3

***In your best handwriting*, write a few sentences about yourself (your family, hobbies, pets, etc.).**

____

____

____

____

6.4

Look at your writing above. Check how good it is by filling in the chart on page 39. Get a friend to help you.

6.5

Write down two things you could do to make your writing better.

____

____

HANDWRITING CHECKLIST

marks out of ten

A Letters and words are on the line ☐

The other day we

B Non-capital letters are the same size ☐

- -and when we saw -

C There are good spaces between words ☐

it was not long

D Writing is a good size (e.g. not too small) ☐

on the London

E Writing slants the same way ☐

when the train

F Capital letters are clear ☐

Megan and Ashik

G Letters are well formed ☐

a d g n p

H General appearance is good (no smudging, neat crossing out) ☐

siad× said

6.6

You are going to fill in the job application form on the next three pages. When you fill it in, it is going to look the best you can make it.

Note: You will need help, from your teacher or tutor, for this.

FIND THE INFORMATION

1 Read through the form carefully. If there is anything you do not understand, ask your teacher.

2 Ask at home for any more information you need.

- Your National Insurance Number (NI number). If you are 16 or over, you may have been sent a card with it on.
- Make sure you know what to write for 'ethnic origin'.
- Find the names and addresses of two people who will give you a reference.
  - *a)* Someone who has known you a long time, for example your vicar, rabbi, youth club leader, or a friend of the family.
  - *b)* A teacher, or someone you have worked for before.
- Check if you had any illnesses or operations when you were young.

WRITE THE FIRST DRAFT

- Write this on a sheet of paper.
- Work out how small your printing will need to be to look neat. You could trace over some of the places where there is not much room.
- Work out the exams you will be taking. Practise putting this down in the space given.
- Where there is no tick box or YES/NO box, write down an answer, for example, NONE.

6.7

FILL IN YOUR FORM

Do this as carefully as you can. You could write it lightly in pencil first.

APPLICATION FOR EMPLOYMENT

SOMERFIELD

FOOD GIANT

PERSONAL DETAILS Please complete all entries in CAPITAL LETTERS

† MR MRS MISS MS †Delete as appropriate †Marital status ____________

SURNAME

FORENAMES

INITIALS

DATE OF BIRTH • •

ADDRESS

TOWN

COUNTY

POST CODE

NI NUMBER

HOME TELEPHONE NUMBER

PREVIOUS SURNAME

WE ARE AN EQUAL OPPORTUNITIES EMPLOYER

ETHNIC ORIGIN

Somerfield is an equal opportunities employer. In order for us to gather details on the ethnic origins of all †applicants and so to monitor our equal opportunities policy, would you please complete the section below:

I would describe my ethnic origin as ☐ (enter in box letter by description)

a) UK/Irish b) Other European c) African d) Asian e) Oriental

f) Afro-Caribbean g) Other (please specify) ____________________

† **delete** – cross off
† **marital status** – whether you are married, single, divorced, widowed
† **applicants** – people applying for a job

If you have not been in continuous employment over the last **5 years**, please give the names and addresses of two people unrelated to you who would give you a personal reference.

1. Name: ______________________

   Full postal address: ______________________

   ____

   ____

   Occupation: ______________________

2. Name: ______________________

   Full postal address: ______________________

   ____

   ____

   Occupation: ______________________

HEALTH AND FITNESS

What illnesses do you suffer from? ______________________

How many days illness have you had in the past year? ______________________

Date and details of any long period of time off work due to sickness over the past 5 years:

____

Have you ever had a serious accident, illness or operation? **YES/NO** If yes, give details:

____

Are you a registered disabled person? **YES/NO**
If yes, please give Registered Disabled Number ______________________

EDUCATION

Give details of education and skills †acquired since 11, including any examinations passed:

____

____

____

____

____

____

____

____

† **acquired** – gained, got

If you are still at or have just left school/college, please give the name and initials of your Head Teacher/Tutor and the full name and address of your school/college.

____

____

†NEXT OF KIN

Name: ____________________ Relationship : ____________________

Address: ____

Contact telephone number: Day time: ____________________ Home: ____________________

CRIMINAL CONVICTIONS

Have you ever been convicted of a criminal offence other than a minor road traffic offence? **YES/ NO**

If yes, give details: ____

____

GENERAL INFORMATION

Have you a relative in our †employ? **YES/NO** If yes, give details:

Name: ____________________ †Location: __________ Position: ____________________

Do you hold a †current driving licence? **YES/NO**

Give details of any current licence endorsements: ______________________________

____

Have you been employed within Somerfield Group before? **YES/NO**
If yes, enter details below:

Location: ____________________ Position: ____________________

From Date: ____________________ To Date: ____________________

Reason for leaving: ____

____

____

† **next of kin** – your closest relative
† **employ** – employment, working for someone
† **location** – place
† **current** – present, at this time

DELFIELD HOLIDAY CAMP

Keen young people wanted over the summer holidays.

We need help with the following:
- kitchens, dining halls
- caring for the animals
- cleaning house/stables/sheds
- caring for equipment (tents, canoes)
- office work

We can provide transport

Apply in writing to Jane Cliff, 18 Rockside, Nr Shepham, Berks BL4 7KF

6.8

You are going to use page 45 to write a letter for one of the jobs above. They were advertised in the *Times Chronicle* on June 17th. When you write the letter it is going to be the best you can make it.

THE CONTENTS

Work out what you are going to say. Remember:

- Make it clear which job you are applying for.
- Give some details about yourself and why you might be suitable for the job.
- Say you could give good references.
- End with a positive sentence.

WRITE THE FIRST DRAFT

- Write this on a sheet of paper.
- Write out the letter using the same space that you have on page 45. Remember to set it out properly.
- Check for paragraphing, spellings and punctuation.
- Check your handwriting (see pages 38 and 39).

6.9

COPYING THE RE-DRAFTED LETTER

Now copy your letter on to page 45.

UNIT

7 Money, money, money

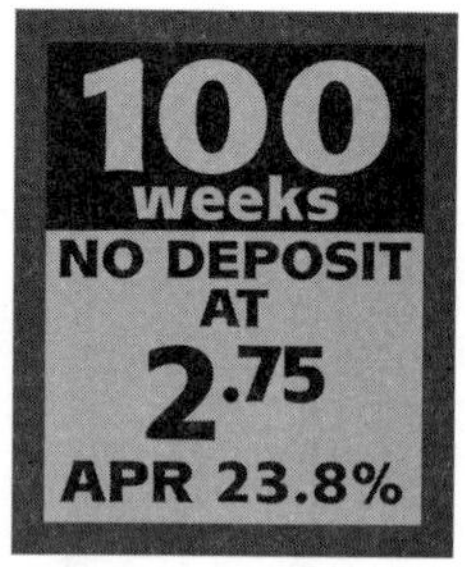

7.1

Read the passage below. Fill in each gap with the word you think best. Try to do this by yourself and not to use the words at the bottom of page 63.

"Do you want a car, a new wardrobe of clothes, a holiday in the sun? Have it now. Pay later." It sounds almost too good to be true and it is.

There are many kinds of credit and lots of ________ are very keen to lend you money. Don't let credit tempt you to ________ something you can't afford. You'll end up ________ much more than if you pay by cash. As well as the cash price you ________ have interest and other charges to ________. Then each week you will lose a ________ of your wages for months or years until you have ________ off the credit.

It may not always be ________ to keep up your repayments. You may lose your ________ or other expenses may crop up. If you get behind with your ________ you'll find it hard to borrow again.

☐ Tick if you did not turn to the back of the book.

HOW MUCH WE SPEND A WEEK
(AVERAGE MONEY SPENT: £283.60)

From *Family Expenditure Survey*

7.2

Read the chart above. Then answer the questions.

1 What does most of the money go on each week?

____

2 How much does the average household spend on clothes and shoes a week?

____

3 How much could be saved in an average household, if everyone gave up smoking and drinking alcohol?

____

4 Which part of the chart would money for holidays be in?

____

5 How many households were questioned for this survey?

____

6 One very important expense has not been filled in. What do you think it is?

____

Mirror firm shows success

A MIRROR-MAKING FIRM that started from a petty-cash tin has become the image of success. It produces eight tonnes of looking-glass goods each week.

And the person who started it all is reflecting on the possibility of expanding into fresh markets.

Mr Evan Watson, of Watson's Glass and Mirrors, Stafford Street, Wolverhampton, set up the firm in 1988. He began with a petty-cash tin and two employees.

Now he has moved to bigger premises and he employs twelve people.

Mr Watson said: "We have just had an order for 2000 mirrors."

"We make designs of every shape and size, and we are planning to expand. We want to sell to furniture and shop-fitting companies."

A reflective moment for Mr Evan Watson

Adapted from: *The Birmingham Post*

7.3

Read the article above. Then answer the questions.

1 What is the business described in the article above?

____

2 How many people did Mr Watson have working for him when he started the business?

---

3 How many people does he have working for him now?

---

4 Where did Mr Watson keep his money when he first started?

---

5 Where do you think Mr Watson keeps his money now?

---

6 Mr Watson hopes to expand into the furniture business. Write down two items of furniture that he might help to make.

7.4

SB

PAGES 94–99

Write out the following, putting in punctuation and capital letters. Set it out as you think best.

dear mr mills i am writing to say that i would like to cancel the standing order of £40 that is paid monthly to jenkins and sons my account number is 93704471 and the number of the standing order is 011879645 yours sincerely

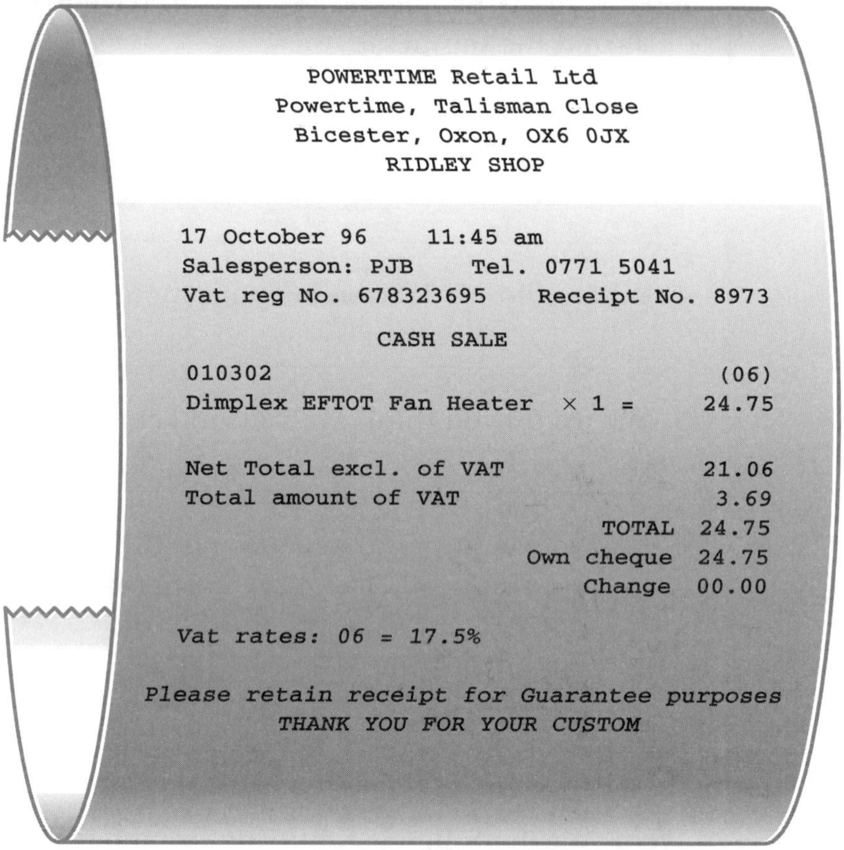

POWERTIME Retail Ltd
Powertime, Talisman Close
Bicester, Oxon, OX6 0JX
RIDLEY SHOP

17 October 96   11:45 am
Salesperson: PJB   Tel. 0771 5041
Vat reg No. 678323695   Receipt No. 8973

CASH SALE

010302	(06)
Dimplex EFTOT Fan Heater × 1 =	24.75
Net Total excl. of VAT	21.06
Total amount of VAT	3.69
TOTAL	24.75
Own cheque	24.75
Change	00.00

Vat rates: 06 = 17.5%

Please retain receipt for Guarantee purposes
THANK YOU FOR YOUR CUSTOM

receipt – a written proof that something has been paid for
excl. – excluding, not counting or taking into account
VAT – **V**alue **A**dded **T**ax, a tax that is sometimes added to a bill
retain – keep
guarantee – a promise to replace the goods if something goes wrong

7.5

Read the details on the receipt above. Then answer the questions.

1 *a)* What did the customer buy?

____

b) On what date and at what time did the customer buy it?

____

____

2 *a)* What sum of money did the customer pay the shopkeeper?

____

b) How much of that money was to pay for the VAT?

____

3 What letters on the receipt stand for the person who served the customer?

____

4 What is the number of this receipt?

____

5 Why is it a good idea to keep the receipt?

____

____

7.6

The customer is not happy with the way the heater is working. With a highlighter or coloured pen, underline the details on the receipt that the customer would need to give in a letter of complaint.

7.7

SB
PAGES
60–61

Write out the cheque that the customer would have filled in on that day. The cheque would have been made payable to Powertime. Use your own name.

BARCLAYS

20-99-93

HIGH STREET, CAXTON, LONDON, N99 4XX

19

Pay *or order*

£

J M ENGLAND

SPECIMEN

BARCLAYS BANK PLC

Cheque No. *Branch No.* *Account No.*

543047 209993 01234567

UNIT 8 Accidents

999 emergency

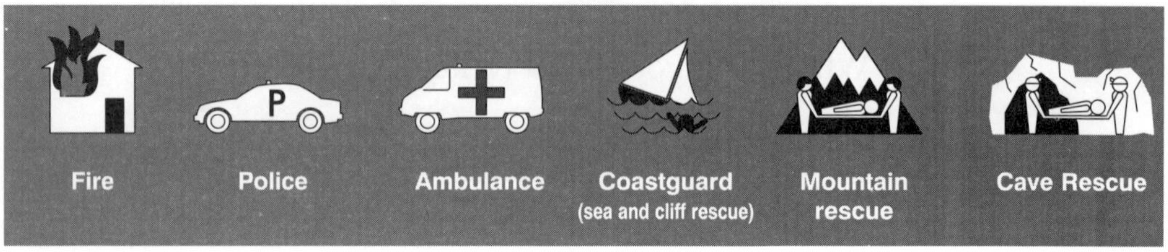

8.1

The instructions below tell you how to make an emergency telephone call, but they are in the wrong order. Work out the order you think they should be in. Write down your answers by putting the numbers 1–5 in the boxes.

A. Tell the Emergency Service: ☐
a) what the trouble is
b) where it is
c) where you are telephoning from.

B. Tell the operator which Emergency Service you want. ☐

C. You may be asked for the number of the telephone you are using. ☐

D. Lift the telephone handset and press or dial 999. ☐

E. Wait for the BT (**B**ritish **T**elecom) operator to connect you to the emergency service. ☐

8.2

The words in the instruction below are in the wrong order. Write out the instruction putting the words in the order you think best.

make call a Never false. lives It help the of need others really could risk who.

____

____

8.3

Read the passage below. There are ten words missing. Fill in the gaps with the words you think best. Try to work this out for yourself and not to use the words at the bottom of page 63.

Children who are lost or who have an emergency can find help at their fingertips if they know how to use the phone. Teach your child how to dial a phone number.

Train your child how to use 100 (Operator) or ____________ (Emergency Services). Teach your child their last name ____________ your first and last names. If the child is ____________ enough, teach them your home phone number and ____________ .

Instruct your child ____________ to tell callers that you are not at home. Ask the child to say that you are busy; please ____________ back later. If the child is old enough, tell them to take a____________ . Teach your child who is a stranger and ____________ isn't. Just as we don't get into ____________ with strangers, we don't give strangers information over the ____________ .

☐ Tick if you did not have to turn to the back of the book for help.

8.4

Using the information below, fill in the form opposite as if you were the line manager. Use your own address.

On October 22nd 1996 Jade Singer slipped in the corridor outside her office in room 21 of the Emerald Insurance building, where she worked as a secretary for Miss Dean. She was not carrying anything when the accident happened. She fell awkwardly, breaking her leg and bruising her back and one arm. The time was 2 pm.

A colleague, Mr Wilks, saw her fall and came rushing to help her. He found that her left leg was twisted but could see nothing that could have caused the accident. He called for help, then made her as comfortable as he could. The line manager, Mrs Simm, phoned for a doctor, who came very quickly.

Miss Singer was sent to hospital where she had an X-ray and her broken leg was treated. She was able to go home on the same day. However, she took a week off work to recover from the shock.

Mrs Simm returned to the corridor and found that there was some wax on the floor where Miss Singer had fallen. Miss Singer said later that she had not seen anything on the floor, but suddenly her right foot had slipped and she had fallen over. Mrs Simm scraped some of the wax from the floor and it was found to be polish left by the cleaners.

Miss Singer was 23 years old and her payroll number was 43/30.

ACCIDENT FORM

TO BE COMPLETED IN ALL CASES OF INJURY OR ACCIDENT AT WORK

DATE OCCURRED

TIME OCCURRED (24-HOUR CLOCK)

FULL NAME (Surname first).. Age..........

STAFF/PAYROLL no..

OCCUPATION.. LINE MANAGER..

ADDRESS..

....

NORMAL PLACE OF WORK..

PLACE WHERE ACCIDENT OCCURRED..

WHAT HAPPENED (In detail)..

....

....

WITNESS/ES (Give details)..

....

....

PLEASE TICK RELEVANT BOXES

	✓
FIRST AID WAS GIVEN	
DOCTOR ATTENDED	
ATTENDED HOSPITAL FOR TREATMENT ONLY	
ATTENDED HOSPITAL FOR MORE THAN 24 HOURS	
ATTENDED HOSPITAL FOR OBSERVATION ONLY	

Tick: Main cause to which injury relates	✓	**Injuries received**	✓	**Parts of body affected**	✓
Fall from a height		Burn/scald		Head	
Fall, slip – same level		Cuts/scratches		Chest	
Struck by object/s		Bruising/swelling		Abdomen	
Stepping against objects		Sprains/strains		Back	
Hot substances, chemical		Fracture/break		Arm	
Handling, lifting, carrying		Shock, no injury		Leg	
Other		Other		Other	

COMMENTS (any further details e.g. cause of accident)..

....

....

Signature (Line manager)..

NO. OF DAYS ABSENT FROM WORK ☐ STILL ABSENT ☐

8.5
SB
PAGES
115–118

Some completed accident claims have to be filed away. The names of the people involved are written below: 1–9. Work out where these names should go in each of the files below. Then write down the names in the correct order in the file. Take care to copy the names correctly. The first one has been done for you.

The names to be filed.

1 Boden K. L. ✓	**2** Mensah F. S.	**3** Herbert O. J.
4 Krawczyk A. J.	**5** Thomas L. B.	**6** Gallagher S. A.
7 Thomas T. W.	**8** Bowen D. V.	**9** Heslop J. H.

A–C	**D–Hes**
Boden K. L.	

Het–Nol	**Nom–Rev**

Rew–Tom	**Ton–Z**

Getting together

UNIT 9

9.1

SB PAGES 94–99 104–106

This is a reply to a wedding invitation. Write it out again putting in the punctuation and capital letters. Set it out as you think best.

dear curtis and belle thank you for the invitation for georgie's wedding i am so sorry to have to tell you that we will not be able to come the doctors have decided to send josh to the great ormond street hospital in london his first day there is the day of the wedding we have sent georgie a wedding present have a lovely day sal and trevor

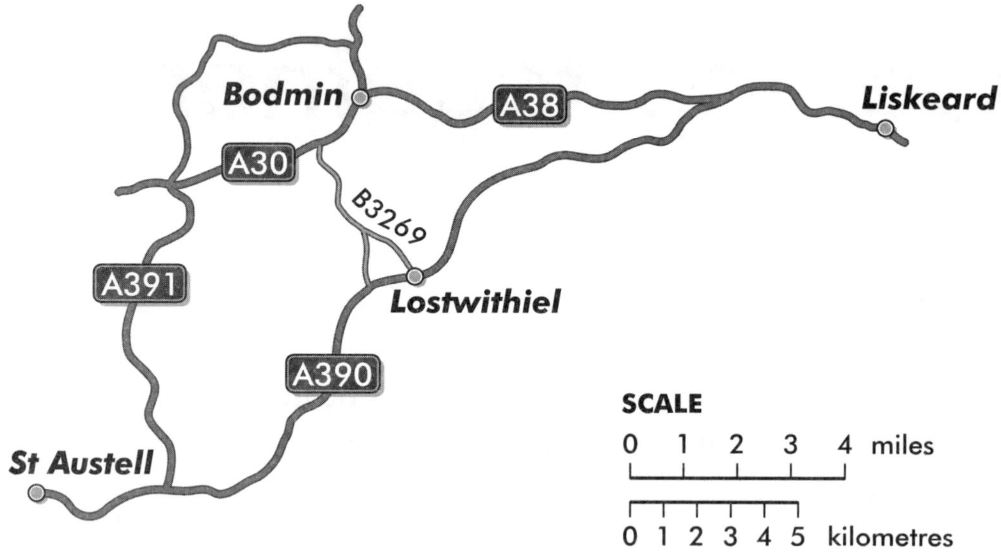

9.2

Tam and Jason are giving a party. They live in Lostwithiel. Look at the map above carefully, then answer the questions below.

1 Some friends live in St Austell.

a) Give the number of the road that they will travel on to Lostwithiel.

____

b) About how many miles or kilometres will the journey be to the party?

____

2 During the party there is an argument. Some friends who live in Liskeard say they had further to travel to get to the party than the people living in St Austell. Who was right?

____

____

3 Some friends who live in Bodmin usually go to Lostwithiel on the B3269. This road is closed on the night of the party. They find there are two other routes, A and B. Describe each route giving directions, road numbers and approximate distances.

Route A Bodmin to Lostwithiel	**Route B Bodmin to Lostwithiel**
______________________	______________________
______________________	______________________
______________________	______________________
______________________	______________________
______________________	______________________
______________________	______________________
______________________	______________________
______________________	______________________
______________________	______________________
______________________	______________________

9.3

Imagine you are giving a party for twenty friends. Make a list of some of the things you will need to do to get ready for the party.

____

____

____

____

____

____

____

~*Community Awards*~

If you know of anyone in your area who you think deserves praise, fill in the attached form. Perhaps your next-door neighbour spends most of the time helping others; perhaps your favourite football team raises money for charity. No one is too young or too old to win an award. So get thinking.

Winners will receive a cash prize of £500 plus a trophy. If the person or group you choose is given an award, you will also profit and receive £50.

Nomination form

I would like to nominate:

Name ______________________________

Address ______________________________

For the award of:

Man of the Year	Woman of the Year	Neighbour of the Year	Team of the Year
❐	❐	❐	❐

Tick the box which is applicable

Give details of why you think your nomination should win the award:

____

____

____

____

____

Your name and address: ______________________________

____

____

Your signature: ______________________________

community – people who live in the same area
to nominate – to put forward someone's name

9.4

Read all the details on page 60. Then answer the questions.

1 What is the form for?

____

____

2 What would the person or group have to do to win an award?

____

____

3 Where would the person or group have to live?

____

4 How much money would they win?

____

5 How much money would you win if you nominated the winning person or group?

____

9.5

Write down the name of someone you could nominate. If you do not know anyone in your area, pick someone from somewhere else. Use the space below to jot down some of the things you could say about him or her.

____

____

____

____

9.6

Now fill in the form opposite using your notes above.

Chapter Two

Achievement chart

When you have finished this book, you will have evidence of achievement in the following areas. Use the tick boxes to help track your progress.

	Pages	
• reading timetables	4 ☐	
• punctuation: capital letters, paragraphs	5 ☐	21 ☐
	49 ☐	57 ☐
• using alphabetical order	13 ☐	31 ☐
	56 ☐	
• understanding and filling in forms	22 ☐	40–43 ☐
	55 ☐	60 ☐
• understanding newspaper articles	6 ☐	48 ☐
• sequencing the alphabet and months of the year	34 ☐	38 ☐
• reading maps	9 ☐	29 ☐
	58 ☐	
• building your vocabulary	23 ☐	24 ☐
	27 ☐	43 ☐
	50 ☐	61 ☐
• filling in blanks	10 ☐	17 ☐
	46 ☐	53 ☐
• understanding abbreviations	4 ☐	20 ☐
	28 ☐	31 ☐
• writing a job application letter	44–45 ☐	